AF223602

LYING LIPS

MORALLY ACCEPTABLE
OR SIN?

Lying lips are an abomination to the LORD, But thos who deal truthfully are his delight
Proverbs 12:22

M J Richards

Cover design and illustration: Michael Richards
Divider designed by Kjpargeter / Freepik

Unless otherwise noted, Scripture quotations are taken from the Holy Bible, King James Version (KJV)—Public Domain.

Passages marked ESV are quoted from The Holy Bible, English Standard Version® (ESV®)
© 2001 by Crossway, a publishing ministry of Good News Publishers.
All rights reserved.

Verse on front cover taken from the New King James Version®. Copyright © 1982 by Thomas Nelson. Used by permission. All rights reserved.

Typeset in Aileron

First Edition
Book 1 of The Commandment Series

ISBNs:
978-1-7643453-5-4 — Hardcover
978-1-7643453-2-3 — Softcover
978-1-7643453-4-7 — E-book
978-1-7643453-6-1 — Audio book

Published by: Orthos Publications

TABLE OF CONTANCE

PREFACE ....*i*

SECTION ONE ....*v*

ABSOLUTELY MORAL 1

PRINCIPLE OR PREFERENCE 12

THE NINTH COMMAND 21

LYING IN THE LIGHT OF SCRIPTURE 29

THE END JUSTIFIES THE MEANS? 37

DEEPER THAN YOU THINK 49

SECTION TWO **59**

RAHAB 61

THE HEBREW MIDWIVES 69

DAVID 75

SAMUEL 79

HIDING JEWS 83

SECTION THREE **91**

DANIEL & FRIENDS 93

NATHAN & DAVID 99

JOSEPH IN EGYPT 103

THE BIBLE'S CALL TO HONESTY 107

SECTION FOUR **113**

STANDING IN THE TRUTH 115

AFTERWORD 121

SECTION FIVE **123**

APPENDIX A 125

APPENDIX B 127

APPENDIX C 135

APPENDIX D 139

SCRIPTURAL CONCORDANCE 141

NOTES 149

PREFACE

Lying. It comes naturally to us as human beings. We all do it, whether in significant or small ways. When someone asks how our week has been or how we're doing, we often give the polite answer they expect rather than the truth.

"I'm good, thanks," slips out of our mouths almost by habit. Yet if we are honest, none of us can honestly say we are good.

...there is none good but one, that is, God. (Mark 10:18)

We lie to many people, strangers, colleagues, friends, and even family. Our children grow up in a world filled with falsehoods. Consider the story of Santa Claus. We know it isn't true, yet we say, "If you're not good, Santa won't bring you presents." When in reality it is a lie, no matter how innocent it may seem. Santa has never given anyone gifts; he isn't real.

These examples might appear harmless, but they reveal something deeper about the human heart. If we are willing to lie in small things, what about greater ones? What about lying to save a life? How many of us would say, "Of course, it's only a little white lie"?

But what makes a lie white or black, good or bad? Could there be such a thing as a righteous lie? And more importantly, what does God say about it?

This book is the result of a personal search for those answers. What began as an attempt to merely defend an idea became a journey to provide, not just a debate, but a balance. By God's grace, I have realised that truth isn't just a subject to debate; it is a Person to be known and a principle to be lived out.

My prayer is that as you read, you'll be inspired to reflect on your own heart and to explore the Scriptures for yourself.

May each of us cultivate a love for truth, speak it in love, and reflect the One who is "the way, the truth, and the life."

SECTION ONE

THE FOUNDATION

CHAPTER ONE
ABSOLUTELY MORAL

Many people in our world today believe there are no absolutes. It is being taught in schools and universities. This idea of questioning everything and that there can't be any form of absolutes, as everything is relative. Moral relativism, often supported by the assumption that there is no Creator, has its roots in a worldview shaped by the evolutionary theory, which teaches survival of the fittest. In such a framework, moral worth is subjective rather than absolute.

However, if there are no absolutes and we have evolved, merely trying to survive in a world where people's worth doesn't exist, laws become a matter of preference rather than principle. This ultimately leads to chaos because one person's idea of morals differs from another's, resulting in a lack of unity and peace.

Take the Holocaust, for example. During World War II, millions of Jews and other minorities were systematically murdered under Adolf Hitler's regime. Even today, the horrors committed by the Nazis are universally condemned as evil. But if there are no moral absolutes—if right and wrong are just personal or cultural preferences—then on what basis can we say that what the Nazis did was wrong? After all, in their own eyes, they believed they were justified.

But something deep within tells us that this was not just "wrong for us," but wrong in an absolute sense.

This collective moral outrage indicates that there is a universal law inscribed on the human heart—a law that transcends time, culture, and personal opinion.

We all have an intrinsic sense of right and wrong, and it's no coincidence. Whether you're a Christian or not, believe in evolution or creation, you can't help but acknowledge that there is deep within us something that tells us right from wrong.

This deep sense of justice isn't random. It's a universal imprint—a conscience that speaks to something greater. I believe that 'something greater' is God. The God who, from the beginning, declared our worth by saying, "Let us make man in our image." (Gen. 1:26). Think about it! An eternal God coming down and wanting to create something in his image.

Since God created us in His image, let's start by looking at the foundation of God's character. We find this foundation laid out in Exodus chapter 20—the Ten Commandments.

Are they absolutes? Some argue that they have been done away with or fulfilled, and we are discharged from the law. However, there is no evidence in scripture to support the idea that the Ten Commandments have been done away with, fulfilled, or that we are discharged from them. There is, however, plenty of evidence in favour of the commandments being absolute and unchangeable.

Let's start by looking at two things. If God's law were ever to change, one could conclude that:

1) God is not trustworthy, as He is subject to change; and

2) Since He is subject to change, He is not absolute.

Yet, the Bible does not support this way of thinking. Malachi 3:6 says, "For I am the LORD, I change not..." God does not change; He is "the same yesterday, today, and forever" (Heb. 13:8). He remains consistent, which is relieving in a world that so often lacks consistency.

Not only does God remain constant, but we also find evidence for the unchangeability of the commandments. One significant piece of evidence is no surprise—God is unchanging. Since the commandments are a transcript of His character[1], His commandments cannot change.

The Bible clearly describes God's law as unchanging and enduring forever,

> ...all His commandments are sure. They stand fast forever and ever, and are done in truth and uprightness (Ps. 111:7-8).

The commandments are done in truth and

---

[1] See Appendix A

uprightness. In other words, truth and right doing underpin each command.

Furthermore, there was never a time when His law did not exist, and there will never be a time when His law will cease to exist.

His law even existed in heaven before sin!

> *Because the law worketh wrath: for where no law is, there is no transgression (Rom. 4:15).*

If there were no law in heaven, why was Lucifer judged a sinner? For where there is no law, there is no sin. *The Review and Herald* put it this way.

> *The moral law was never a type or a shadow. It existed before man's creation and will endure as long as God's throne remains.*[2]

Further evidence for an unchanging law is found in Matthew 5:18, which says,

---

[2] *The Review and Herald*, April 22, 1902

For verily I say unto you, Till heaven and earth pass, one jot or one tittle shall in no wise pass from the law, till all be fulfilled.

Fulfilled means:

> *...to become, to take place, to be established. God will not modify or alter His expressed will. His word will accomplish His beneficent purpose and prosper (Isa. 55:11). There will be no change in the divine precepts to bring them into conformity with man's will.*[3]

Once again, God's law has not changed, does not change, and will not change throughout all eternity.

Let's revisit the objection regarding being discharged or set free from the law. Allen Walker, in his book *The Law and the Sabbath*, explains,

> *These words, 'discharged from the law' [referring to Rom. 7:6], are legal terms. A man pays another man's penal-*

---

[3] *Seventh-day Adventist Bible Commentary 5, 1956, p.333*

ty, and the judge says to the prisoner, 'You are discharged, sir.' He does not mean discharged to go out and violate the law again, but discharged from the penalty. So on the cross, Christ paid our penalty and thus made it possible for us to be discharged from the law as far as its death penalty was concerned. Then we become 'dead [to that] wherein we were held,' namely, the death penalty...

To clarify that he was not arguing that the law is 'dead' and no longer operative against the transgressor, Paul says, 'What shall we say then? Is the law sin? God forbid. Nay, I had not known sin, but by the law: for I had not known lust, except the law had said, Thou shalt not covet.' (Rom. 7:7). How could any commandment of a dead law condemn a living man for violating it? Such a thing would be impossible. But the very fact that Paul quotes the Tenth Commandment of the Sinai law and goes on to say that it is this law that reveals a knowledge of sin—this positively proves it was still in force and very much alive (pp. 31-32).

Once again, the law remains valid and un-changed. It is absolute!

This world is subject to constant change; values, laws, and truths are ever-evolving. However, the unchanging character of God offers stability and assurance. His law is a blessing; it's a clear standard that maintains justice, exposes sin, and highlights our need for a Saviour. Unlike the disorder of moral rel-ativism, the Ten Commandments depict a God who cares about you. They are more than just rules inscribed on stone; they reflect the character of the God who gave them, and because He is absolute, His law is absolute.

Wherefore the law is holy, and the com-mandment holy, and just, and good. (Rom 7:12)

Thought Questions

1. According to the chapter, what evidence does Scripture give that God and His law never change?

2. How does the chapter explain the relationship between God's character and the Ten Commandments?

3. What difference would it make in your own life if you lived as though God's law were truly absolute?

CHAPTER TWO

PRINCIPLE OR PREFERENCE

Because God's law is unchanging, how we relate to it is profoundly important. The next question we need to ask is simple but essential: Is God's law a principle we are meant to live by, or just a preference we can choose to follow or ignore?

To better understand this question, it is helpful to note the meaning of these two words.

The word principle means:

A fundamental truth or proposition that serves as the foundation for a system of belief or behaviour or for a chain of reasoning.[1]

So, a principle underpins belief, behaviour, or reasoning.

On the other hand, preference means:

The act of preferring one thing before another; estimation of one thing above

---

[1] *Oxford English Dictionary,* 1857

another; choice of one thing rather than another.[2]

The difference lies in one [principle] being a foundation and the other [preference] being an option or choice. In other words, if there is a principle, you can only work within the boundaries set by that principle. If you have a preference, you have many options. If you dislike an option, you can opt out or choose an alternative, as no fundamental principle binds you.

The Bible includes numerous principles. For instance, the principle of a day for a year in Ezekiel 4:6 aids in understanding biblical prophecies, as without this principle, we would be very lost in our understanding of the topic. Similarly, Isaiah outlines a principle for studying the Bible, and if we do not follow it, we will find ourselves down a rabbit hole of wrong interpretations. There are many more Bible principles, but they are not our subject for this chapter.

Consider the law of the land as an example.

---

[2] *Noah Webster's 1828 Dictionary*

Is it a principle or merely a preference? Imagine a driver caught speeding in an 80 km/h zone. When asked why, he replies, "I prefer to drive at 100." Does his preference override the law? If the law were not a principle, then yes, but it is. So the result is a fine.

Laws, by their nature, operate as principles—break them, and there are consequences.

Let's consider how God framed His law. Is it a preference? Can we choose to abide by one part of His law and not another? Or is it a principle, a fundamental truth setting the foundation for our belief and even existence? Did he present them as options?

His law is the foundation of His government. It has been under attack ever since Lucifer sinned. If it were simply a matter of preference, why is it subjected to so much opposition? The very fact that it faces such resistance indicates that it is more than just a preference.

But let's now look at how the commandments have been written. We don't need to examine every commandment in detail to see the pattern. A few are enough to make the principle clear.[3]

- The first commandment says, "Thou shalt have no other gods before me" (Ex. 20:3). The language used indicates that it is more than a suggestion; it's a direct, non-negotiable command. *Thou shalt not.* Deuteronomy 11:27-28 confirms this with the reality of consequence: "A blessing, if ye obey... and a curse, if ye will not obey."

- The fourth commandment, concerning the Sabbath, is equally firm: "Remember the sabbath day, to keep it holy... In it thou shalt not do any work" (Ex. 20:8-10). Once again, you have the language of the verse indicating a principle with a *thou shalt not.* Exodus 31:14 confirms that it is a principle by listing the existence of consequences, "everyone that defileth it shall surely be put to death."

- The ninth commandment—our focus

---

[3] See Appendix B for more on this subject.

in this book—follows the same pattern: "Thou shalt not bear false witness against thy neighbour" (Ex. 20:16). Like the others, it is phrased as a principle. It assumes authority and carries consequence. As we'll see, this commandment goes far beyond courtroom testimony.

We must not treat God's law as something optional, for it is a reflection of who He is: eternal, righteous, holy, just, and good. To lie, then, is not merely to break a rule—it is to misrepresent the very character of God.

Ultimately, lying is an attack on the very character of God, for it contradicts who he is.

To lie is to rebel against God Himself.

If the law is a principle, why then are we not seeing consequences for breaking it? Although judgment doesn't always fall immediately, as in the Old Testament, that doesn't mean it is forgotten. The Bible assures us:

He will make an utter end: affliction shall not rise up the second time (Nah. 1:9).

This is both a warning and a promise. One day, justice will be fully served, and every sin accounted for.

But here's the good news: judgment is not the end of the story.

The same law that exposes our sin also points us to our Saviour. For "the law was our schoolmaster to bring us unto Christ, that we might be justified by faith" (Gal. 3:24). When the law shows us our guilt, it is not to crush us; it is to point us to Christ.

Jesus did not come to abolish the law but to fulfil it (Mat. 5:17); to live it out perfectly, so that he could offer His righteousness to those who have broken His law, and ultimately to prove Satan a liar.

The commandments, then, are not cold rules, but divine principles of love and truth. They are rooted in God's unchanging character. And because God is love, His law is love too (Rom. 13:10).

Preference often replaces principle today, yet God's law still stands. It offers a standard we can trust, a mirror to examine ourselves by, and a path that leads us to Christ.

God's law is not a preference; it is a principle.

Praise God, in Christ, we find the power to walk in truth.

> *But as many as received him, to them gave he power to become the sons of God, even to them that believe on his name. (John 1:12)*

Thought Questions

1. What distinction does the chapter make between a principle and a preference?

2. How does the chapter show that God's commandments operate as principles rather than optional preferences?

3. In what areas of your life might God be calling you to move out of principle rather than preference?

CHAPTER THREE
THE NINTH COMMAND

Having established that the law of God is an absolute principle, we can now approach the issue of lying not as a matter of personal preference but as a moral principle.

With this foundation established, we are more equipped to understand what it means to bear false witness and its importance to God.

The ninth commandment says,

> *Thou shalt not bear false witness against thy neighbour (Ex. 20:16).*

Seems simple, right? Not necessarily, because some try to justify lying by claiming that there are grey areas in this commandment and that it is perfectly acceptable to lie in certain situations.

But this raises the question: if the commandment is a principle and a moral absolute, both of which have been established thus far, how can there be grey areas?

The answer to this question will become clearer as we examine the Bible for guidance in the following chapters.

But let's look at what it means to bear false witness. At its core, it refers to giving a misleading or dishonest testimony, deliberately misrepresenting the truth.

For example, if you retell a story from an event you attended but exaggerate it by adding details that never happened, you've borne false witness.

Others, though, will argue that this command is solely for a court of law and therefore doesn't apply to us when it comes to general lying. I would agree that, yes, it does apply to bearing testimony in a court of law, but it extends even further. Leviticus 19:11 says,

> *Ye shall not steal, neither deal falsely, neither lie one to another.*

This verse addresses lying in a general sense, not just in a court setting. It begins with principle language, *ye shall not*, then uses *neither*. You can properly exchange the word *neither* with the phrase *ye shall not* without altering the meaning. In that case, it would read, "Ye shall not steal. Ye shall not deal falsely. Ye shall not lie one to another." This affirms that one should not lie to anyone.

This concept of general lying is not limited to the Old Testament; It is also found in the New Testament:

> *Lie not one to another, seeing that ye have put off the old man with his deeds (Col. 3:9).*

This passage provides further insight into why lying is wrong. The reason is that we have *put off the 'old man' with his deeds.*

To understand the insight given in Colossians, we must first ask: Who is the *old man,* and what are his deeds?

It's simple: the *old man* is the body of sin—the life lived before conversion. Paul writes,

> *Knowing this, that our old man is crucified with him [Christ], that the body of sin might be destroyed, that henceforth we should not serve sin (Rom. 6:6).*

From this, we learn two things:

1. The *old man* is crucified so that the body of sin might be destroyed.

2. Because the *old man* is crucified, we are no longer to serve sin.

What is sin? "Sin is the transgression of the law" (1 John 3:4). So, as long as the old man is alive and uncrucified, we remain in transgression of God's law.

Ephesians 4:22 reinforces this point:

Put off concerning the former conversation the old man, which is corrupt according to the deceitful lusts.

Immediately afterwards, Paul explains the solutionary replacement to this *old man*:

"Be renewed in the spirit of your mind" (v. 23), and *"Put on the new man, which after God is created in righteousness and holiness of truth" (v. 24, margin).*

This new man reflects true righteousness, or

right-doing, and holiness of truth, not a worldly form of holiness—a hypocritical holiness that is only a front to make oneself look good —but one that is honest, one that does not put up a lying front.

To make this unmistakably clear, Paul continues:

> *Wherefore putting away lying, speak every man truth with his neighbour: for we are members one of another (v. 25).*

In other words, as long as we are lying, the old man remains alive; we are not living in the new life of truth.

At this point, someone might ask, "But doesn't that only apply to how we treat our neighbours? What about those who aren't part of the faith or aren't close to us?"

In answering this question, we must ask: Who is our neighbour?

Jesus was asked the same question in Luke 10:25-37, when a lawyer asked Him what one must do to inherit eternal life. In verse 29 —right after he answered Jesus' question about what the law was—the lawyer, seeking to justify himself, asked, "And who is my neighbour?"

In response, Jesus told the story of the Good Samaritan—a man who helped a wounded stranger left for dead. At the end of the parable, Jesus asks, "Which now of these three, thinkest thou, was neighbour unto him that fell among the thieves?" The lawyer answered, "He that showed mercy on him." Jesus then replied, "Go, and do thou likewise" (verses 36–37).

The point is clear: our neighbour is anyone we come into contact with, regardless of race, religion, or relationship.

So, if Paul says not to lie to our neighbour, and Jesus says everyone we meet is our neighbour, then lying is never acceptable.

There are no exceptions.

We are called to speak the truth to everyone! But we can only achieve this with the power of Christ working in and through us.

Provide things honest in the sight of all men. (Rom. 12:17)

Thought Questions

1. According to the chapter, what does it mean to "bear false witness" beyond the context of a courtroom?

2. How does Paul's teaching about the "old man" and the "new man" explain why lying cannot exist in the life of a Christian?

3. What habits or forms of speech in your life might God be asking you to surrender to the truth?

LYING IN THE LIGHT OF SCRIPTURE

God's law remains unchanged, and in Christ, it becomes a promise of what He can accomplish in us. One of those promises is truthfulness. To understand how seriously God takes this, we must carefully examine what He says about lying throughout Scripture.

Let's begin by asking a question: If God is truth, where did lying originate?

Jesus made it clear in John 8:44(ESV):

> *...the devil...was a murderer from the beginning, and does not stand in the truth... for he is a liar, and the father of lies.*

Lying comes from Satan, not from God. If lying originated with God, we would see examples of Him lying; however, the truth is, we don't. In fact, the Bible plainly says that He cannot lie.

> *"In hope of eternal life, which God, that cannot lie, promised before the world began." "God is not a man, that he should lie."*

Jesus Himself said, *"I am the way, the truth, and the life"(Titus 1:2; Num. 23:19; John 14:6).*

Lying was the very tool Satan used in the Garden of Eden when he claimed Eve would not die if she ate of the tree. That is the lie that introduced sin into our world.

This, then, raises the question: if lying originates with the devil, why then would God be pleased with our lying? It's one of the very sins that caused Satan and a third of the angels to be cast out of heaven.

Continuing with a Biblical explanation of lying, in Psalm 58:3, it is depicted as something the wicked engage in:

The wicked are estranged from the womb: they go astray as soon as they are born, speaking lies.

Furthermore, Psalm 101:7-8 highlights that individuals who engage in deceit and lie will face destruction.

He that worketh deceit shall not dwell

within my house: he that telleth lies shall not tarry in my sight. I will early destroy all the wicked of the land...

Let's explore this further.

Thou lovest evil more than good; and lying rather than to speak righteousness (Ps. 52:3).

This verse presents two parallel ideas. Just as evil is set in contrast to good, so lying is set in contrast to speaking righteousness. In this way, the verse identifies lying as evil and truth-telling as good. The two are moral opposites.

Lying is not just a bad habit; it is the very opposite of righteousness.

The Bible also explicitly condemns lying as an abomination.

This is emphasised in Proverbs 12:22,

Lying lips are an abomination to the LORD: but they that deal truly are his delight.

The term *abomination* means *extreme hatred or detestation*.[1] This strong language reveals just how deeply God detests lying. If God perceives lying as morally objectionable, should we then assume His approval of it in specific circumstances? The answer is un-equivocally no.

While He loves us profoundly, He abhors the sin of falsehood.

The Bible consistently depicts lying as some-thing negative, and I haven't come across any case where it's shown positively or with-out repercussions.

In the end, those who are righteous will ab-hor lying. It will be deemed unattractive, even when one's life or someone else's is at stake.

> *A righteous man hateth lying: but the wicked man is loathsome, and cometh to shame (Pro. 13:5).*

This hatred of lying is not born of self-right-eousness, but of transformation (2 Cor. 5:17).

---

[1] Noah Webster's 1828 Dictionary

As Christ writes His law in our hearts (Jer. 31:33), the things that once seemed normal or justifiable begin to repel us. As the old song says,

> *And the things of earth will grow strangely dim, In the light of His glory and grace.*[2]

In Christ, truth becomes more than a moral demand; it becomes the natural outflow of a heart renewed by Him—a reflection of His character written within.

> *The law of his God is in his heart; none of his steps shall slide (Ps. 37:31).*

---

[2] *Turn Your Eyes upon Jesus,* Helen Howarth Lemmel (1922)

Thought Questions

1. Where does the Bible say lying originated, and how does that contrast with God's nature?

2. Why do you think God views lying as an abomination?

3. How might understanding God's hatred of lying deepen your desire to reflect His truth?

CHAPTER FIVE

THE END JUSTIFIES THE MEANS?

From the previous chapters, we've seen clearly three things:

1. God's law is absolute

2. It is a principle, and

3. Lying has no place in the life of a righteous person. It does not align with the character of God or the foundation of His government.

Yet many still lie. Instead of confronting the sin, we often seek to excuse it—even when the truth is clear and accessible. Why do we seek answers that oppose the clear teachings of Scripture?

Sometimes, lying appears more straightforward, especially when the truth seems costly or inconvenient. We're afraid of what honesty might bring: loss, rejection, or hardship. So we reason that a small lie might spare us or others from a worse outcome. This is the beginning of the belief that the end justifies the means.

The philosophy that *the end justifies the*

means holds that if the result is good, then the actions taken to achieve it—whether right or wrong—are acceptable. In this framework, success is the standard for righteousness, not obedience. But Scripture teaches that the standard of righteousness is obedience, not outcome.

This mindset may not always be obvious. It shows up in subtle reasoning: "God understands—I had no other choice." But what if the means you use to achieve a 'good' end are evil in God's eyes? Can a bad tree produce good fruit?

Scripture directly confronts this logic. Paul questions why he should be judged a sinner if the truth of God supposedly thrived through his lie.

> *But if through my lie God's truth abounds to his glory, why am I still being condemned as a sinner? And why not do evil that good may come?*
> *(Rom. 3:7-8 ESV).*

Even if the outcome is positive, he is still guilty of sin. In other words, doing the wrong thing, even for a supposedly right reason, is still wrong.

Our dishonesty does not glorify God. A lie is never righteous, no matter how noble the cause.

A clear example of this *end-justifies-the-means* thinking is presented in the life of King Saul. In 1 Samuel 15, Saul was instructed by God to annihilate the Amalekites, including men, women, children, and animals. However, after gaining the victory, Saul chose to spare the king and the best of the sheep, oxen, fatlings, lambs, and all the good things. They only destroyed what was "vile and refuse" (1Sa 15:9).

This went against God's clear command. Although, to make an already bad situation worse, Saul lied to the prophet Samuel:

> *...and Saul said unto him, Blessed be thou of the LORD: I have performed the commandment of the LORD (1Sa 15:13).*

Samuel confronts Saul by asking what the meaning of the animal sounds are, to which

Saul continues to lie by blaming the people for taking them to sacrifice to the Lord.

Saul's theory was essentially this: "If I keep the good things for a sacrifice, then I can disobey God's command." In other words, the end justifies the means.

Samuel goes on to tell Saul that he has done evil in the sight of the Lord. Again, Saul repeats the lie, saying the people have taken the spoil, not him, and that it was for a good cause.

Then Samuel says:

> *Behold, to obey is better than sacrifice, and to hearken than the fat of rams. For rebellion is as the sin of witchcraft... (1Sa 15:22-23).*

Obedience is far better than sacrifice. Samuel even goes so far as to say that the rebellion—the willful disobedience of God's clear commands—is the same as witchcraft!

God would rather we obey than sin to achieve a moral goal.

In the end, Saul repented out of fear of the consequences, and because his repentance was not genuine, God rejected him as king. It reminds me of a quote from a book I read recently, which said:

> *Sometimes we feel that we have to sin our way out of the consequences of sin —by lying or hiding the truth—and it all snowballs into an unimaginable disaster.*[1]

We, too often like Saul, see the great wrong we have done and where our sin is leading and attempt to escape the consequences by lying.

So let's bring this to today with a practical example. Some might ask, "What about lying to save innocent lives, like hiding Jews during the Holocaust?" If telling the truth might result in your death and the inevitable death of others, can lying be permissible?

---

[1] Sam Allberry, *Why does God care who I sleep with?* p.77

This question is often framed as the ultimate *grey area*. But again, the foundation laid earlier remains firm.

I'm not saying these questions are irrelevant or don't deserve thoughtful answers, but they shouldn't lead us to reinterpret the character of God or His law. Scripture teaches us that truth never changes, even when the stakes are high.

God's law does not bend for circumstance. As a Pastor friend of mine once put it, when building a fence, you don't bend all the straight posts to match the bent one; instead, you bend the bent one to align with the straight ones. And it's the same with truth; you don't approach a seemingly grey area and try to bend the clear commands of God to fit the grey area; instead, you adjust the grey area to align with the clear commands of God.[2]

We will look at some examples of hiding Jews and how God worked mightily through

---

[2] I'm grateful to my friend, Pastor Dana Howard, for sharing this example.

honesty in our next section. But something to keep in mind when looking at this question is a verse from Mark 13, which says:

But when they shall lead you, and deliver you up, take no thought beforehand what ye shall speak, neither do ye pre-meditate: but whatsoever shall be given you in that hour, that speak ye: for it is not ye that speak, but the Holy Ghost (v. 11).

This is an important verse to remember. It applies to many of these situations. If we want to speak the truth, we should allow the Holy Spirit to speak through us.

This is where faith and fear come into play. Fear drives us to grasp for control, and it's in these moments that we believe the only way to stay safe and survive is to lie. Why? Because we're afraid of what might happen if we tell the truth.

On the other hand, faith hands control over to God in every situation, even when we can't see how the truth will win.

Something that goes hand in hand with faith is love. 1 John 4:18 says:

There is no fear in love; but perfect love casteth out fear: because fear hath torment. He that feareth is not made perfect in love (1 John 4:18).

If we truly love God, we will have faith in Him, even when the cost of obedience appears high. Jesus said, "If ye love me, keep my commandments" (John 14:15). Fear should not produce obedience; it should be the fruit of love.

God is infinitely powerful! We need not intervene; God knows what He is doing. He does not need our lie to 'help' him; He needs our trust.

The commandments are not to be bent to suit our circumstances; they are to shape our choices. God calls us to stand still and see His salvation. And when we genuinely believe that "God is for us" (Rom. 8:31), fear loses its grip.

It can be hard to find our footing in a world

where the idea that the end justifies the means is both familiar and compelling. But God is not impressed by outcomes gained through compromise. He is not looking for excuses, results, or a "well-meaning" lie. What He desires is a heart that trusts Him enough to choose what is right, regardless of the cost.

There is a way which seemeth right unto a man, but the end thereof are the ways of death (Pro. 14:12).

Thought Questions

1. How does the chapter use the story of King Saul to demonstrate that doing wrong for a good reason is still sin?

2. What does 1 Samuel 15:22-23 reveal about God's view of using evil means to achieve good outcomes?

3. When have you been tempted to compromise truth for convenience, and what might trusting God look like in that moment?

CHAPTER SIX

DEEPER THAN YOU THINK

Lying runs deeper than most realise. It's not always as obvious as a bald-faced lie. There are subtle forms or layers of deception that, unless carefully examined, can slip by unnoticed. To truly understand the importance of the ninth commandment, we need to look beyond the surface.

Thus far, we have laid a solid biblical foundation. The Bible clearly states: "These six things doth the LORD hate: yea, seven are an abomination unto him... a lying tongue... a false witness that speaketh lies..." (Proverbs 6:16-19). God doesn't just discourage lying; He hates it. And this hatred isn't limited to spoken falsehoods but extends to all kinds of deception, including subtle or socially accepted forms.

Author Ellen G. White offers profound insight into the depth of this commandment. While some may not be familiar with White's writings, her explanation reflects the broader biblical standard of integrity found throughout Scripture.

The essence of lying, as she defines it, is the intent to deceive, whether through words, gestures, silence, or implication.

> *False speaking in any matter, every at-*
> *tempt or purpose to deceive our neigh-*
> *bour, is here included. <u>An intention to</u>*
> *<u>deceive is what constitutes falsehood.</u>*[1]

Jesus rebuked the Pharisees not for their words but for their actions—appearing truthful on the outside while hiding falsehood within.

> *Even so ye also outwardly appear right-*
> *eous unto men, but within ye are full of*
> *hypocrisy and iniquity (Mat. 23:28).*

In other words, hypocrisy is a form of falsehood in which external appearance conflicts with internal truth.
White continues:

> *By a glance of the eye, a motion of the*
> *hand, an expression of the countenance,*
> *a falsehood may be told as effectually as*
> *by words.*[2]

---

[1] Ellen G. White, Patriarchs and Prophets, 1890, p. 309

[2] Ibid.

This principle reaches into areas we might not expect, such as entertainment. The word *actor* itself historically refers to someone who behaves in a way that is not genuine.[3]

Whether in film or theatre, depicting a false reality for entertainment raises significant moral questions.

White's commentary expands our understanding of lying, showing it isn't limited to spoken words but also includes misleading gestures, omissions, causing injury to others by suppressing the truth, and facial expressions.

However, in a society focused on appearances, the urge to showcase an idealised image of ourselves has grown stronger. This prompts a key question: Is it possible to deceive others not just through words, but also through our manner of presentation?

I'm not condemning all forms of personal care or grooming, but I'm addressing inten-

---

[3] Oxford English Dictionary, 1857

tional misrepresentation and questioning the intentions behind how we present ourselves.

Are we trying to come across as something we're not—whether it's youth, wealth, etc.—in a way that misleads others about our true character?

The Bible offers cautionary examples:

- 2 Kings 9:30 says, "And when Jehu was come to Jezreel, Jezebel heard of it; and she painted her face, and tired her head, and looked out at a window." This was a last-ditch effort to assert influence through appearance.

- Paul instructed women to "adorn themselves in modest apparel, with shamefacedness and sobriety" (1 Tim. 2:9).

- Peter urged, "Whose adorning let it not be that outward adorning… but the hidden man of the heart" (1 Peter 3:3-4).

The principle in each passage is consistent:

outward display must not become a tool for deception. Whether through acting, silence, implication, or cosmetics, anything that deliberately misrepresents is a form of falsehood.

This does not apply only to women; it applies equally to men.

White continues:

> *All intentional overstatement, every hint or insinuation calculated to convey an erroneous or exaggerated impression, even the statement of facts in such a manner as to mislead, is falsehood.*[4]

This also calls us to examine how we present information. Even when the facts are technically accurate, if they are arranged to mislead or manipulate perception, we cross into the realm of falsehood.

And what about silence? She warns that "Even the intentional suppression of truth, by which injury may result to others, is a viola-

---

[4] Ellen G. White, Patriarchs and Prophets, 1890, p. 309

tion of the ninth commandment."[5] Imagine someone falsely accused while we withhold the truth that could clear their name; our silence then becomes a form of deception.

The implications are sobering. We may be guilty of breaking the ninth commandment more often than we realise. James 2:10 reminds us:

Whosoever shall keep the whole law, and yet offend in one point, he is guilty of all.

The story of Ananias and Sapphira in Acts chapter 5 serves as a solemn reminder of God's view on lying. They sold land and gave part of the money to the apostles, claiming it was the entire amount they had agreed upon. Their deception was intentional and straightforward, leading to both of them being struck dead. The core issue was not the sum they donated, but their attempt to mislead by a lie.

This story illustrates that dishonesty, even in

---

[5] Ibid.

acts of generosity or during religious service, remains a sin that God cannot overlook.

Why did God respond so severely? To protect the integrity of the early church and to warn against hypocrisy in sacred things.

Christ requires nothing short of obedience to the law's commands. Let us not deceive ourselves into thinking that lying applies only to spoken words.

Thought Questions

1. What forms of deception does the chapter identify beyond spoken lies?

2. What does genuine honesty look like in your everyday interactions and presentation of yourself?

SECTION TWO
ANSWERING OBJECTIONS

CHAPTER SEVEN
RAHAB

A familiar story is that of Rahab, who hid the Israelite spies to save them from certain death. This story is often used to suggest that lying can be justified in some situations. But was it right for her to lie? Did God save her because of her lie? And is the Bible endorsing lying to save a life?

Let's revisit the story in Joshua chapter 2. Joshua sent two men to spy out the land, and they found refuge in Rahab's house, a harlot who lived in defiance of God's law[1].

When the king was informed, he sent men to Rahab's house[2]. Rahab met these men and tricked them by lying, saying that the spies had already left the city[3]. This lie diverted the pursuers, saving the lives of the two spies.

Initially, lying seemed to serve a noble purpose and helped save lives. We know that Rahab asked the spies to protect her and her family when they came to destroy the city. As a result, Rahab and her household were

---

[1] Verse 1

[2] Verses 2-3

[3] Verses 4-5

spared. But does this mean God approved of saving a liar? A more thorough look is needed.

The first thing to note is that Rahab was a heathen at that time, and lying wouldn't have seemed wrong because she didn't know any better.

Secondly, diverging from Rahab's story, we need to consider who God saves and what standard of living one must follow for salvation. At first glance, it seems God spared a lying prostitute, but Matthew 1:21 sheds light on this:

> *And she shall bring forth a son, and thou shalt call his name JESUS: for he shall save his people from their sins.*

Jesus doesn't save us *in* our sins, but *entirely from* them. The term *from* suggests that after Jesus saves you from sin, you are no longer under its control.

Consider this: being saved from death means you get to live. Similarly, being saved from sin implies freedom from its power, resulting in a life characterised by righteousness and purity.

Another significant verse, 1 Thessalonians 5:23, highlights God's wish for total sanctification:

> And the very God of peace <u>sanctify you wholly;</u> and I pray God your <u>whole spirit and soul and body be preserved blameless unto the coming of our Lord Jesus Christ.</u>

Sanctification involves dedicating oneself to God and separating from sin, thereby ensuring a blameless life until Christ's return.

Considering these verses[4], it is clear that God does not save people who are entrenched in sin. He saves those who have been transformed.

Rahab indeed turned from her former ways. A well-known Christian author comments,

> All who, like Rahab the Canaanite and

---

[4] More verses in Appendix D

Ruth the Moabitess, turned from idolatry to the worship of the true God were to unite themselves with His chosen people.[5]

Rahab's faith spared her from destruction. Through faith, Rahad did not meet the same fate as those who did not believe.

A similar transformation occurred with the thief on the cross, who acknowledged his sinfulness and earnestly sought Jesus.

But the other answering rebuked him, saying, Dost not thou fear God, seeing thou art in the same condemnation? And we indeed justly; for we receive the due reward of our deeds: but this man hath done nothing amiss (Luke 23:40-41).

A man who was once a robber and opposed to Christ now recognises his sinful condition and his need for a saviour. And he sees in Jesus his salvation.

God does not save sinners in their sin but

---

[5] Ellen G. White, Prophets and Kings, 1917, p. 19

rescues them, leading to a transformed life free from sin's bondage.

Returning to Rahab's story, it's evident that although she initially lied, she later repented.

An interesting thing to note, though, is that every time the Bible talks about Rahab and the reason why she was saved, it never mentions her lie. It only ever mentions that she was saved because she took the spies in or sent the spies away, but never because she lied.

> *By faith the harlot Rahab perished not with them that believed not, when she had received the spies with peace. (Heb. 11:31)*

> *And in the same way was not also Rahab the prostitute justified by works when she received the messengers and sent them out by another way? (James 2:25 ESV)*

This clearly demonstrates that when the Bible recounts stories like this, it is descriptive rather than prescriptive.

In conclusion, Rahab's example demonstrates that God saves those who repent and turn away from their sins. Salvation involves transformation, and not condoning sin. Once the sin is revealed, repentance is required.

And the times of this ignorance God winked at; but now commandeth all men everywhere to repent (Acts 17:30).

CHAPTER EIGHT

THE HEBREW MIDWIVES

Many believe that the Hebrew midwives lied to Pharaoh and were blessed for it. But is that what Scripture says? Did God reward a lie?

The story is found in Exodus 1:16-20, where Pharaoh instructed the midwives to kill all male babies that were born.

> *But the midwives feared God, and did not as the king of Egypt commanded them, but saved the men children alive.*

When questioned by Pharaoh, they said:

> <u>*Because the Hebrew women are not as the Egyptian women; for they are lively, and are delivered ere the midwives come in unto them.*</u> *Therefore God dealt well with the midwives... because the midwives feared God, that he made them houses (v. 17-21).*

At first glance, it seems that the Hebrew midwives lied to Pharaoh, and God blessed them for it. However, a closer examination is necessary.

Adam Clarke, a respected 19th-century Bible

scholar, offers a detailed perspective on this very point. He suggests that rather than lying, the midwives were stating a truth Pharaoh could have easily verified, and that this honesty stood in sharp contrast to his cruelty.[1]

Clarke writes:

> *The Hebrew women are not as the Egyptian women - This is a simple statement of what general experience shows to be a fact...*

He explains that women accustomed to physical labour often experience quicker childbirth, and given the Israelites' harsh slavery (Ex. 1:14), this explanation is plausible.

Clarke continues:

> *...with the strictest truth the midwives might say... the Hebrew women are lively... and therefore are delivered ere the midwives come in unto them.*

---

[1] See Appendix C for full commentary.

Rather than fabricate a story, Clarke argues, they described what Pharaoh himself could easily verify. If they had lied, he could have investigated and punished them. But he didn't.

Clarke concludes:

> *Here then is a fact, boldly announced in the face of danger... and we see that God was pleased with this frankness of the midwives, and he blessed them for it.*

In other words, the midwives weren't being deceptive; they were being brave. And God rewarded their courage, not their falsehood.

Clarke recounts an experience he saw:

> *I saw a poor woman in the open field at hard labor; she stayed away in the afternoon, but she returned the next morning to her work with her infant child, having in the interim been safely delivered! She continued at her daily work, having apparently suffered no inconvenience!*

This account supports the plausibility of the

midwives' claim. Their explanation to Pharaoh was not a cunning fabrication but a genuine reflection of what Clarke—and likely others—had personally seen among women accustomed to physical labour. Instead of lying to protect themselves, the midwives told the truth and entrusted the outcome to God.

The story of the midwives invites us to ask: When faced with pressure to compromise truth, do we stand with integrity as they did?

Honesty is not just about avoiding lies—it's about trusting that God can bless truthfulness, even when it seems risky.

> *The lip of truth shall be established for ever: but a lying tongue is but for a moment (Pro 12:19).*

CHAPTER NINE
DAVID

In 1 Samuel 21, David approaches the priest and, driven by fear, fabricates a story to obtain bread and Goliath's sword. This instance involving David underscores the significance of truthfulness in all circumstances, as his lie resulted in the death of innocent people.

Adam Clarke comments on verse 2:

All said here is an untruth, and could not be dictated by the Spirit of the Lord; but there is no reason to believe that David was under the influence of Divine inspiration at this time. It is well known that from all antiquity it was held no crime to tell a lie, in order to save life. Thus Diphilus:

'I hold it right to tell a lie, in order to procure my personal safety; nothing should be avoided in order to save life.'

A heathen may say or sing thus; but <u>no Christian can act thus, and save his soul, though he by doing so may save his life.</u>

Clarke's commentary draws a clear distinction between the worldly philosophy of self-preservation at any cost and the Christian call to truth, even in times of crisis. While ancient cultures excused lying to save life, Scripture holds God's people to a higher standard.

David's deception was not divinely inspired; it was a moment of weakness, not faith. The outcome was devastating, and it reminds us that fear-driven falsehood always bears bitter fruit.

Ellen G. White likewise reflects on the cost of David's fear-driven decision. She writes:

> *The young man was in constant fear of discovery, and in his extremity, he resorted to deception... In doing so, he displayed a lack of faith in God, and his wrongdoing led to the tragic death of the high priest. If the truth had been plainly stated, Ahimelech would have known how to safeguard his life. God demands that His people exemplify truthfulness, even in the face of grave danger.*[1]

David's lie had severe repercussions. After

---

[1] Patriarchs and Prophets, 1890

discovering that Ahimelech the priest had unknowingly helped David, King Saul ordered his execution. When Saul's servants refused to carry out the order, Doeg the Edomite was sent to do it (1 Sam. 22:18).

David's story clearly illustrates how a single lie, even under pressure, can lead to widespread suffering and bloodshed. It also reminds us that God values truth over cleverness and faith over fear.

Behold, thou desirest truth in the inward parts: and in the hidden part thou shalt make me to know wisdom (Ps. 51:6).

CHAPTER TEN
SAMUEL

Some argue that God once told the prophet Samuel to lie. This raises the question: Can God command someone to do what He condemns? If we've already seen that "God... cannot lie" (Titus 1:2), and that truth is the foundation of His government, how do we reconcile this claim? Does the story of Samuel anointing David reveal divine deception, or is something else going on?

In this chapter, we'll examine the passage closely.

The story is found in 1 Samuel 16:1-5, the Lord instructs Samuel to anoint David as king. Fearful that Saul, the king, will discover his intentions and kill him, Samuel asks God, "How can I go?" The Lord responds by advising him to take a heifer and tell all who ask that he is there to offer a sacrifice to the Lord. At first glance, it appears that God instructed Samuel to lie about his plans. However, we must delve deeper into the story to determine if this conclusion is accurate.

The text never shows Samuel speaking lies.

As we continue reading from verse 4, we see

that Samuel faithfully followed the Lord's instructions. He took a heifer with him and sacrificed just as God instructed him. Did he need to disclose the entirety of his plans? No.

If I go to the shop to buy milk and also pick up flowers for my wife, saying "I'm going to buy milk" is still truthful. Not every purpose must be announced for a statement to be honest.

The difference between a lie and discretion is the intent. What was left unsaid was not intended for deception because the information was neither owed nor necessary in the context.

Jesus Himself counselled discretion in Matthew 10:16, saying, "Be ye therefore wise as serpents, and harmless as doves."
Christ withheld His identity in His trial until He was asked under oath. Was He lying by not answering the questions?

Samuel's declaration that he had come to sacrifice was entirely accurate. His silence about anointing David did not make him dishonest; there was no intention to deceive; it was a wise concealment in a time of danger, not a breach of truth.

God cannot lie (Heb. 6:18), and therefore He cannot command someone to lie on His behalf. His instructions to Samuel were not deceitful; they were careful, purposeful, accurate, and most importantly, led by God.

> *He is the Rock, his work is perfect: for all his ways are judgment: a God of truth and without iniquity, just and right is he (Deut. 32:4).*

CHAPTER ELEVEN
HIDING JEWS

Some argue that telling the truth, even when hiding Jews or in other life-and-death situations, is morally wrong. But from the Bible's perspective, lying is never justifiable. "Lying lips are abomination to the LORD: but they that deal truly are his delight" (Proverbs 12:22). God doesn't need us to bend the truth to achieve His will.

When we justify deception to "protect" others, we are essentially saying, "God, I don't trust You with this outcome—I'll take control instead." But faith chooses obedience and leaves the outcome in God's hands, even if it's frightening or uncertain.

Consider two real examples, the first of which is from the book *The Hiding Place* (1971) by Corrie Ten Boom, which illustrates what God can accomplish when the truth is spoken:

They jerked the table back, snatched away the rug, and tugged open the trapdoor. Bob lowered himself first, lying down flat, and Peter tumbled in on top of him. We dropped the door shut, yanked the rug over it, and pulled the table back in place. With trembling hands, Betsie,

Cocky, and I threw a long tablecloth over it and started laying five places for tea...

...Cocky stared at him a second, then dropped her eyes. My heart stood still. I knew how Nollie had trained her children—but surely, surely now of all times a lie was permissible!

'Do you have brothers?' the officer asked again.

'Yes,' Cocky said softly. 'We have three.'...

...'Where are they now?' the soldier persisted.

Cocky leaned down and began gathering up the broken bits of cup. The man jerked her upright. 'Where are your brothers?'

'The oldest one is at the Theological College. He doesn't get home most nights because—

'What about the other two?'

Cocky did not miss a breath.

'Why, they're under the table.'

Motioning us all away from it with his gun, the soldier seized a corner of the cloth. At a nod from him, the taller man crouched with his rifle cocked. Then he flung back the cloth.

At last, the pent-up tension exploded: Cocky burst into spasms of high hysterical laughter. The soldiers whirled around. Was this girl laughing at them?

'Don't take us for fools!' the short one snarled.

Furiously he strode from the room and minutes later the entire squad trooped out—not, unfortunately, before the silent soldier had spied and pocketed our precious packet of tea.

It was a strange dinner party that evening, veering as it did from heartfelt thanksgiving to the nearest thing to a bitter argument our close-knit family had ever had. Nollie stuck by Cocky, insisting she would have answered the same way. 'God honours truth-telling with perfect protection!'

The second example is drawn from the book *A Thousand Shall Fall* (2001) by Susi Hasel Mundy, when they hid a Jewish boy:

For several days, all remained quiet. Then one afternoon, Helene answered the doorbell to three men dressed in long black leather coats — the Gestapo. 'Frau Hasel,' they began without preliminaries, 'you are under suspicion of hiding a Jew in your apartment. We have a search warrant. You know what will happen to you and your family if we find him.' It was a statement, not a question.

'Now we are asking you, are you hiding a Jew?'

Confused thoughts shot through Helene's mind. Will God forgive a lie if it can save the boy and us? If I tell the truth, we are all lost. Lord help me!

Stepping out of the way, she finally stammered, 'If you want to, you may search my apartment.'

'Frau Hasel,' the men asked again, 'are you hiding a Jew?'

Again, Helene invited them to search the apartment.

A third time they asked, 'Tell us, are you hiding a Jew?'

Opening the door wide, Helene motioned to the men. 'Feel free to search the apartment.'
The men looked at each other. Then without another word, they turned and left.

A few days later, the underground picked the boy up and moved him to safety in the country where he survived the war.

These testimonies demonstrate that God's way remains the best, even when it appears perilous. Speaking the truth in tough times doesn't always yield the results we want, but it ensures we act with integrity and trust God with the rest.

> *But if not, be it known unto thee, O king, that we will not serve thy gods... (Dan. 3:18)*

SECTION THREE

EXAMPLES OF HONESTY

CHAPTER TWELVE

DANIEL & FRIENDS

A story familiar to many is that of Daniel and his friends, who were taken to Babylon. And that right from the start,

> *Daniel purposed in his heart that he would not defile himself with the portion of the king's meat, nor with the wine which he drank (Dan. 1:8).*

From the beginning, Daniel and his friends chose to start well and decided to trust in God for all their needs and wants. This purpose remained true as we see later in their lives.

Starting with Daniel's three friends, we have a perfect example of honesty and integrity in times of danger. When King Nebuchadnezzar commanded all to worship a golden image, Shadrach, Meshach, and Abednego refused to do so.

They could have lied by their actions and bowed down, praying to God instead, but they chose to stand boldly and remain faithful to God.

They were brought before the king, who offered them a final chance to bow or face death in a fiery furnace.

They boldly replied:

God whom we serve is able to deliver... But if not... that we will not serve thy gods, nor worship the golden image which thou hast set up (Dan 3:17, 18).

Furious, the king ordered the furnace heated seven times hotter and had them thrown in. Yet instead of perishing, they were seen walking unharmed in the flames with a fourth figure "like the Son of God" among them. Nebuchadnezzar called them out, and not even the smell of fire was on them.

Moved by their faith, the king praised their God and promoted them. Their uncompromising honesty and loyalty to truth brought not only deliverance but also glory to God.

Next, Daniel faced a similar test. He had distinguished himself as an honest and capable leader under King Darius, which stirred jealousy among the other officials. Unable to find any fault in him, they plotted against his faith.

They convinced the king to pass a law forbidding anyone but the king from praying for 30 days, knowing Daniel would remain faithful to his God.

Again, Daniel could have lied by action and either closed his window to prayer or prayed somewhere else, yet despite the threat, Daniel continued praying three times a day, just as he had before. Caught in the act, he was brought before the king, who, though distressed, was bound by the unchangeable law of the Medes and Persians. Daniel was cast into the lions' den.

God honoured Daniel's honest faith. He sent His angel to shut the lions' mouths, and Daniel was unharmed. The next morning, a relieved Darius found Daniel alive. In response, the king punished the conspirators and issued a decree that all should honour the God of Daniel, who "delivereth and rescueth... who hath delivered Daniel from the power of the lions." (Dan. 6:27)

Daniel's integrity and unshakable trust in God not only preserved his life but also brought glory to God throughout the kingdom.

These two stories underscore the vital importance of truthfulness and integrity in all situations. These men chose to honour God above self-preservation, trusting Him with the outcome. Their unwavering stance not only preserved their character but also served as a powerful witness to a watching world.

Whether before kings or under threat of death, God honours those who choose what is right over what is easy.

CHAPTER THIRTEEN
NATHAN & DAVID

King David has just sinned against God, Bathsheba, and Uriah. God tells Nathan, the prophet, to rebuke him. This story illustrates how speaking the truth—guided by trust in God—can bring both conviction and healing. We find this story in 2 Samuel 12.

Nathan told David a parable about a rich man who stole a poor man's only lamb to feed a guest, instead of using one from his large flock. David, angered by the injustice, declared, "As the LORD liveth, the man that hath done this thing shall surely die:" (v.5) and must repay fourfold.

David has unknowingly sentenced himself to death by answering the prophet's question. Nathan now faces a choice: tell the truth and risk being killed—since David is king and has the power to do so—or withhold the truth to stay in David's favour, yet disobey God.

Nathan, being a faithful prophet, did not shrink from the truth, even though confronting a king could have cost him his life. He said, "Thou art the man," exposing David's sin. He reminded David of all God had given him and rebuked him for despising God's commandment. Because of his actions, David was told that violence would never leave his house and that what he had done in secret would be repaid openly.

After hearing Nathan's words, David confessed, "I have sinned against the Lord." Nathan assured him that God had put away his sin and he would not die, but warned that the child born from this affair would die as a consequence.

Nathan's courage reminds us that honesty is not always safe, but it is always the right thing to do.

CHAPTER FOURTEEN

JOSEPH IN EGYPT

Joseph's story stands as a powerful example of truthfulness in the face of pressure and temptation. Sold into slavery by his brothers and brought to a foreign land, Joseph could have allowed bitterness or compromise to shape his decisions. Instead, even as a servant in Potiphar's house, he distinguished himself by faithfulness and integrity. Potiphar trusted him so completely that he "left all that he had in Joseph's hand" (Gen. 39:6).

But this trust brought its own test. Day after day, Potiphar's wife tried to seduce him. She was persistent and demanding. Yet Joseph refused her advances, not only out of loyalty to his master but with a greater principle in mind: "How then can I do this great wickedness, and sin against God?" (v. 9).

Eventually, she grabbed his garment and demanded that he lie with her. Joseph fled, choosing righteousness over self-preservation. Yet for this act of integrity, he was falsely accused and thrown into prison. Honesty led not to honour but to disgrace. He lost his position, his reputation, and his freedom. But he kept something far more valuable: his conscience was clean before God.

Joseph's story reminds us that honesty doesn't always yield immediate rewards. Sometimes, like Joseph, we suffer for doing what's right. The reward for integrity is often delayed, but never denied. In time, God exalted Joseph.

Joseph's life challenges us: Will we be honest even when no one is watching? Even when it costs us dearly? Will we trust that God sees and will reward faithfulness in His own time?

CHAPTER FIFTEEN

THE BIBLE'S CALL TO HONESTY

To gain a balanced approach to this issue, we must examine honesty as it is presented in scripture.

A well-known verse goes like this:

> *Finally, brethren, whatsoever things are true, whatsoever things are honest, whatsoever things are just, whatsoever things are pure, whatsoever things are lovely, whatsoever things are of good report; if there be any virtue, and if there be any praise, think on these things. (Phil. 4:8)*

This verse encourages us to think only on that which is true, honest, just, pure, lovely, and of good report; all of which relate to truthfulness and honesty.

Paul also emphasises the importance of honesty among those who are not Christian. "Having your conversation honest among the Gentiles: ..." (1 Pet. 2:12)

Another verse worth mentioning is found in Romans 12. "Recompense to no man evil for evil. Provide things honest in the sight of all men." (v. 17) In other words, evil is not speaking honestly, and on top of that, we are to provide honesty in the sight of <u>all</u> men, not just when we feel like it.

In Proverbs, we find, once again, that truthfulness is right and wickedness is its opposite. "For my mouth shall speak truth; and wickedness is an abomination to my lips." (Pro 8:7)

Paul once again states that the truth is to be spoken. "Wherefore putting away lying, speak every man truth with his neighbour: ..." (Eph. 4:25)

We also find that the Godhead is one of truth and honesty.

• The Father: "He is the Rock, his work is perfect: for all his ways are judgment: a God of truth and without iniquity, just and right is he." (Deut. 32:4)

• The Son: "Jesus saith unto him, I am the way, the truth, and the life: no man cometh unto the Father, but by me." (John 14:6)

- The Holy Spirit: "Howbeit when he, the Spirit of truth, is come, he will guide you into all truth: ..." (John 16:13)

In every way, God is a God of honesty; He "...cannot lie..." (Titus 1:2) "...I the LORD speak righteousness, I declare things that are right..." (Isa. 45:19)

The Bible's definition of truthfulness covers all aspects of human activity. Whether in finances, friendships, business, or family, honesty is the key principle that maintains trust and integrity in relationships.

As previously mentioned, Paul wrote, "Provide things honest in the sight of all men" (Rom. 12:17), emphasising that our integrity must be open, visible, and consistent.

For example, the workplace can be a testing ground. Returning extra change at the shop, accurately reporting hours worked, or resisting the temptation to cut corners in a job— these are all tests of whether the principle of honesty guides our actions.

Jesus said, "He that is faithful in that which is

least is faithful also in much" (Luke 16:10). It is not in the big tests but in the quiet, unnoticed ones that our character is formed.

Jesus is our ultimate example. He never compromised, even when honesty led to suffering. When asked if He was the Son of God, knowing that affirming it would lead to the cross, He answered truthfully: "Thou hast said" (Mat. 26:64). His honesty cost Him everything, but He stayed faithful to the end.

A Christian must never sacrifice honesty for ease. Proverbs 28:13 states, "He that covereth his sins shall not prosper: but whoso confesseth and forsaketh them shall have mercy." Covering up sin or wrongdoings with lies means walking away from eternal life. No earthly benefit is worth that compromise.

The moment we believe that telling the truth will cost us too much, we open the door to compromise.

Behold, thou desirest truth in the inward parts: and in the hidden part thou shalt make me to know wisdom (Ps. 51:6).

SECTION FOUR
CONCLUSION

CHAPTER SIXTEEN

STANDING IN THE TRUTH

Lying can be summed up in one word: sin. Whether the intention seems good or bad, lying remains a sin in the eyes of God, no matter who you are or what outcome you hope to achieve.

The Bible is crystal clear: liars will not enter the kingdom of God. Revelation 21:8, 27 warns, "All liars shall have their part in the lake which burneth with fire and brimstone: which is the second death." These are sobering words that cannot be brushed aside.

In the course of writing this book, I have realised just how many times I've lied without even thinking about it—excuses, exaggerations, avoiding the truth under pressure. But there is hope.

Here are a few steps that have helped me:

1. The way forward begins with loving God. As Jesus said, "If ye love me, keep my commandments" (John 14:15). Love is a mighty principle! As 1 John 4:18 states, "... perfect love casts out fear." Wow! The more we love God, the less fear we experi-

ence. And from this love, we are motivated to keep God's commands.

2. Next, we need to build deeper trust in Him. The more we trust God with the outcomes, the less we feel compelled to lie to 'help' God out. Jesus taught, "If ye have faith as a grain of mustard seed, ye shall say unto this mountain, Remove hence to yonder place; and it shall remove; and nothing shall be impossible unto you" (Matt. 17:20). God has given each of us a "measure of faith" (Rom. 12:3). And He is saying that with this faith nothing shall be impossible.

   These two principles define God's final people: the faith of Jesus—faith that even in the face of death, chose to trust God fully—and commandment-keeping. (Rev. 14:12)

3. And finally, we must hide His Word in our hearts. As Psalm 119:11 says, "Thy word have I hid in mine heart, that I might not sin against thee." Memorise scripture; in times of need, the Holy Spirit can bring it to mind.

One scripture that often comes to mind when I face a choice to trust God or sin is 1 Samuel 15:22: "Behold, to obey is better than sacrifice, and to hearken than the fat of rams."

These simple yet powerful principles—love, faith, and the hidden word—can transform how we live and speak.

No matter what the world says, lying is never justified. It is always sin—and through Christ, we can overcome it.

Will you stand for the truth when it's hard, when it's costly, and when no one else does?

Now is the time to decide.

We cannot be effective Christians if we are effective liars.[1]

---

[1] Steve Saunders, *12 Liars in the Bible and the Lives They Ruined*

Thought Questions

1. According to the conclusion, why can truth never be separated from love and faith?

2. How does the book show that lying is not only an act of the lips but a condition of the heart?

3. What step of honesty or repentance might God be calling you to take after reading this book?

AFTERWORD

I began writing this book with the intention of winning arguments, and I believed I had completed it nearly two years ago. However, I was then searching for someone to write a foreword for it. After the first option fell through, I decided to re-read the book. As I read, the Holy Spirit convicted me to make changes, which initiated the process of adding more content and revising it to bring hope to its pages and adopt a more balanced, less argumentative tone.

My aim and prayer for this book is not to win an argument; that's not my role. My role is to present what I believe to be the truth from the Bible and to let you, as the reader, examine it yourself and draw your own conclusions based on the biblical evidence.

I pray you have read with an open mind and are willing to study for yourself so you may "give an answer to every man that asketh you a reason of the hope that is in you with meekness and fear." (1 Peter 3:15)

SECTION FIVE
RESOURCES

APPENDIX A

God's Character	Characteristics of the Law of God
Revelation 16:5; Psalm 7:9; Ezra 9:15. God is righteous.	**Psalm 119:172.** All of God's Commandments are righteousness.
1 Peter 1:16; Deuteronomy 32:4; Mark 10:18. God is holy, just and good.	**Romans 7:12.** The law is holy, just and good.
Exodus 33:18, 19: 34:5-7. God proclaims His name and His character to Moses.	**Exodus 20:5, 6.** God was proclaiming His name/character from the 2nd Commandment.

APPENDIX B

1. **Thou shalt have no other gods before me.**
   1) Deuteronomy 7:4
      a) The anger of the Lord is kindled against you.
      b) Destroyed suddenly.
   2) Deuteronomy 8:19
      a) Forget the Lord thy God and go after other gods.
      b) Ye shall surely perish.
   3) Deuteronomy 11:27, 28
      a) Blessing if the commandments are kept.
      b) Curse if they are not kept.
   4) Deuteronomy 17:3
      a) I have not commanded thee.
      b) v5 They are stoned.
   5) Deuteronomy 29:26
      a) Whom he had not given unto them.
   6) Deuteronomy 31:18
      a) God will hide his face from us.
   7) Judges 10:13
      a) Deliver no more.
   8) Jeremiah 16:11
      a) Not kept my law.
2. **Thou shalt not make unto thee any graven image.**
   1) Deuteronomy 7:25

    a) An abomination to the Lord.
  2) 2 Chronicles 33:19
    a) Graven images lumped in with sin.
  3) Psalm 78:58
    a) Anger and jealousy are the result of graven images.

3. Thou shalt not take the name of the Lord in vain.
  1) Romans 2:21-24
    a) Professing to be a Christian when not living like one.
    b) By your very life, you can take the name of the Lord in vain.

4. Remember the Sabbath day, to keep it holy.
  1) Genesis 2:2-3
    a) Ended his work.
    b) Rested on this day.
    c) Blessed it.
    d) Sanctified it.
  2) Exodus 31:16
    a) It's a perpetual covenant.
    b) Something that is observed or kept.
  3) Exodus 31:13
    a) It is a sign between us and God.
    b) That we may know that he is the Lord that doth sanctify us.
  4) Isaiah 58:13-14

a) Turn from our pleasure.
b) Call the Sabbath a delight, the holy of the Lord.
c) Not doing it our way.
d) Not finding our pleasures.
e) Not speaking our own words.
f) Then the Sabbath will be a delight.
5) Exodus 16:22-26
a) Gather twice as much on Friday.
b) Through the week it rots, but on the seventh day it keeps.
c) 1. It teaches them they should not work on the Sabbath.
d) 2. It's teaching them that the Lord will provide for them.
6) Exodus 31:14
a) Defile the Sabbath, be killed.

5. Honour thy father and thy mother.

1) Ephesians 6:1-3
a) Obey parents, for this is right.
b) First commandment with promise.
c) If we honour and obey our parents, our days will be long in the land that God has appointed for us to live in.
2) "Parents are entitled to a degree of love and respect which is due to no other person. God Himself, who has placed

upon them a responsibility for the souls committed to their charge, has ordained that during the earlier years of life, parents shall stand in the place of God to their children. And he who rejects the rightful authority of his parents is rejecting the authority of God. The fifth commandment requires children not only to yield respect, submission, and obedience to their parents, but also to give them love and tenderness, to lighten their cares, to guard their reputation, and to succor and comfort them in old age. It also enjoins respect for ministers and rulers and for all others to whom God has delegated authority." Patriarchs and Prophets, Ellen G. White, (1958) P. 308.2

6. Thou shalt not kill.
1) Genesis 4
   a) Cain slew Abel.
   b) Cain was driven from the presence of the Lord.
2) Romans 12:19
   a) Vengeance is God's
3) Matthew 26:52
   a) Live by the sword, you will die by the sword.

7. Thou shalt not commit adultery.
   1) Leviticus 20:10
      a) Put to death.
   2) Proverbs 6:32
      a) Destroyeth his soul.
   3) Matthew 5:27-28
      a) Looketh at a woman with lust.

8. Thou shalt not steal.
   1) Exodus 22:1
      a) Restore fourfold.
   2) Proverbs 30:9
      a) Stealing is taking the name of the Lord in vain.
   3) Luke 19:8
      a) Restore fourfold.

9. Thou shalt not bear false witness.
   1) Jeremiah 7:8
      a) Lying words do not profit.
   2) Proverbs 26:28
      a) A lying tongue worketh ruin.
   3) Proverbs 13:5
      a) The righteous hate lying.
   4) Proverbs 12:22
      a) Lying lips are an abomination.
   5) Psalm 59:12
      a) Sin of the mouth.

10. Thou shalt not covet.
   1) Deuteronomy 7:25

    a) It is an abomination.
2) Psalm 10:3
    a) The Lord abhorreth.

APPENDIX C

Adam Clarke, *Commentary on the Bible* (1831)

"The Hebrew women are not as the Egyptian women - This is a simple statement of what general experience shows to be a fact, viz., that women, who during the whole of their pregnancy are accustomed to hard labor, especially in the open air, have comparatively little pain in parturition. At this time the whole Hebrew nation, men and women, were in a state of slavery, and were obliged to work in mortar and brick, and all manner of service In The Field, Exodus 1:14, and this at once accounts for the ease and speediness of their travail. With the strictest truth the midwives might say, The Hebrew women are not as the Egyptian women: the latter fare delicately, are not inured to labor, and are kept shut up at home, therefore they have hard, difficult, and dangerous labours; but the Hebrew women are lively, חיות chayoth, are strong, hale, and vigorous, and therefore are delivered ere the midwives come in unto them. In such cases we may naturally conclude that the midwives were very seldom even sent for. And this is probably the reason why we find but two mentioned; as in such a state of society there could be but very little employment for persons of that profession, as a mother, an aunt, or any female acquaintance or neighbour, could readily afford all the assistance necessary in such cases. Commentators, pressed with imaginary difficulties, have sought for examples of easy parturition in Ethiopia, Persia, and India, as parallels to the case before us; but they might have spared themselves the trouble, because the case is common in all parts of the globe where the women labor hard, and especially in the open air. I have known several instances of the kind myself among the labouring poor. I shall mention one: I saw a poor woman in the open field at hard labor; she stayed away in the afternoon, but she returned the next morning to her work with her infant child, having in the interim been safely delivered! She continued at her daily work, having apparently suffered no inconvenience!

"I have entered more particularly into this subject because, through want of proper information, (perhaps from a worse motive), certain persons have spoken very unguardedly against this inspired record: 'The Hebrew midwives told palpable lies, and God commends them for it; thus we may do evil that good may come of it, and sanctify the means by the end.' Now I contend that there was neither lie direct nor even prevarication in the case. The midwives boldly state to Pharaoh a fact, (had it not been so, he had a thousand means of ascertaining the truth), and they state it in such a way as to bring conviction to his mind on the subject of his oppressive cruelty on the one hand, and the mercy of Jehovah on the other. As if they had said, 'The very oppression under which, through thy cruelty, the Israelites groan, their God has turned to their advantage; they are not only fruitful, but they bring forth with comparatively no trouble; we have scarcely any employment among them.' Here then is a fact, boldly announced in the face of danger; and we see that God was pleased with this frankness of the midwives, and he blessed them for it."

APPENDIX D

The Following list is a compilation of verses that support the statements made in Chapter 7.

1. "God is my strength and power: and he maketh my way perfect." (2 Sam. 22:33)
2. "I in them, and thou in me, that they may be made perfect in one;..." (John 17:23)
3. "That the man of God may be perfect, thoroughly furnished unto all good works." (2 Tim. 3:17)
4. "But let patience have her perfect work, that ye may be perfect and entire, wanting nothing." (James 1:4)
5. "And the very God of peace sanctify you wholly; and I pray God your whole spirit and soul and body be preserved blameless unto the coming of our Lord Jesus Christ." (1 Thess. 5:23)

SCRIPTURAL CONCORDANCE

This Concordance is based on words as they appear in the King James Version. It is not a comprehensive list of words related to lying.

Lie

1. Leviticus 6:2......................................"lie unto his neighbour"
2. Leviticus 19:11................................"lie one to another"
3. Numbers 23:19..............................."that he should lie;"
4. 1 Samuel 15:29................................"Israel will not lie"
5. 2 Kings 4:16....................................."do not lie unto"
6. Job 6:28.."unto you if I lie."
7. Job 34:6.."Should I lie"
8. Psalm 62:9....................."men of high degree are a lie:"
9. Psalm 89:35....................................."that I will not lie"
10. Psalm 119:69................."The proud have forged a lie"
11. Proverbs 14:5................"A faithful witness will not lie:"
12. Isaiah 44:20..................................."lie in my right hand?"
13. Isaiah 63:8......................"children that will not lie:"
14. Jeremiah 27:10..................."For they prophesy a lie"
15. Jeremiah 27:14...................."for they prophesy a lie"
16. Jeremiah 27:15...................."for they prophesy a lie"
17. Jeremiah 27:16...................."for they prophesy a lie"
18. Jeremiah 28:15................................"to trust in a lie."
19. Jeremiah 29:21.......... ...."which prophesy a lie"
20. Jeremiah 29:31................................"trust in a lie:"
21. Ezekiel 21:29.......... ...."they divine a lie"
22. Micah 1:14......................................."shall be a lie"
23. Micah 2:11.......... ...."falsehood do lie,"
24. Habakkuk 2:3.......... ...."and not lie:"
25. Zechariah 10:2.......... ...."have seen a lie,"
26. Jonah 8:44..................................."speaketh a lie,"

27. Acts 5:3.............................."lie to the Holy Ghost,"
28. Romans 1:25.."into a lie,"
29. Romans 3:7..................................."through my lie"
30. Romans 9:1............. ...."I lie not,"
31. 2 Corinthians 11:31.............................."I lie not."
32. Galatians 1:20............. ...."I lie not."
33. Colossians 3:9......................"Lie not one to another,"
34. 2 Thessalonians 2:11..... ...."believe a lie:"
35. 1 Timothy 2:7............. ...."and lie not;"
36. Titus 1:2.."that cannot lie,"
37. Hebrews 6:18.................."impossible for God to lie,"
38. James 3:14......................."lie not against the truth."
39. 1 John 1:6.........................."in darkness, we lie,"
40. 1 John 2:2...................."no lie is of the truth."
41. 1 John 2:27...................................."and is no lie,"
42. Revelation 3:9......................................."but do lie;"
43. Revelation 21:27.........................."or maketh a lie:"
44. Revelation 22:15.............................."maketh a lie."

Lies

1.   Judges 16:10.........................."and told me lies:"
2.   Judges 16:13.........................."and told me lies:"
3.   Job 11:3................"lies make men hold their peace?"
4.   Job 13:4........................"But ye are forgers of lies,"
5.   Psalm 40:4................"nor such as turn aside to lies."
6.   Psalm 58:3..................................."speaking lies."
7.   Psalm 62:4.......... ...."they delight in lies:"
8.   Psalm 63:11.......... ...."lies shall be stopped."
9.   Psalm 101:7................................"he that telleth lies"
10. Proverbs 6:19................................."speaketh lies,"
11. Proverbs 14:5................................."will utter lies."
12. Proverbs 14:25..... ...."speaketh lies."
13. Proverbs 19:5........ ...."speaketh lies"

14. Proverbs 19:9.......... ...."speaketh lies"
15. Proverbs 29:12....................."If a ruler hearken to lies,"
16. Proverbs 30:8........................"from me vanity and lies:"
17. Isaiah 9:15................."the prophet that teacheth lies,"
18. Isaiah 16:6......................"but his lies shall not be so."
19. Isaiah 28:15........................"made lies our refuge,"
20. Isaiah 28:17................................"the refuge of lies,"
21. Isaiah 59:3..................................."have spoken lies,"
22. Isaiah 59:4......................................"and speak lies;"
23. Jeremiah 9:3............"tongues like their bow for lies:"
24. Jeremiah 9:5......................................"to speak lies,"
25. Jeremiah 14:14..............."prophesy lies in my name:"
26. Jeremiah 16:19............................."have inherited lies,"
27. Jeremiah 20:6..................."thou hast prophesied lies."
28. Jeremiah 23:14..............................."and walk in lies:"
29. Jeremiah 23:25..............................."that prophesy lies"
30. Jeremiah 23:26..............................."that prophesy lies?"
31. Jeremiah 23:32............................."to err by their lies,"
32. Jeremiah 48:30............."his lies shall not so effect it."
33. Ezekiel 13:8.."and seen lies,"
34. Ezekiel 13:9............................."and that divine lies:"
35. Ezekiel 13:19............................."that hear your lies?"
36. Ezekiel 13:22..............................."Because with lies"
37. Ezekiel 22:28................................"and divining lies"
38. Ezekiel 24:12........................"wearied herself with lies,"
39. Daniel 11:27..................................."they shall speak lies"
40. Hosea 7:3................. ...."with their lies."
41. Hosea 7:13........................."yet they have spoken lies"
42. Hosea 10:13.......... ...."eaten the fruit of lies:"
43. Hosea 11:12........."compasseth me about with lies,"
44. Hosea 12:1................................."he daily increaseth lies"
45. Amos 2:4....................."their lies caused them to err,"

46. Micah 6:12........................"thereof have spoken lies,"
47. Nahum 3:1.......... ...."full of lies"
48. Habakkuk 2:18............................"a teacher of lies,"
49. Zephaniah 3:13............................"nor speak lies;"
50. Zechariah 13:3................"for thou speakest lies"
51. 1 Timothy 4:2..............."Speaking lies in hypocrisy;"

Lying

1.   1 Kings 22:22..... ...."I will be a lying spirit"
2.   1 Kings 22:23..................."hath put a lying spirit"
3.   2 Chronicles 18:21........................"be a lying spirit"
4.   2 Chronicles 18:22................"hath put a lying spirit"
5.   Psalm 31:6........................."that regard lying vanities:"
6.   Psalm 31:18.................. ."lying lips be put to silence;"
7.   Psalm 52:3........ ...."lying rather than to speak"
8.   Psalm 59:12..................."lying which they speak."
9.   Psalm 109:2.......... ...."with a lying tongue."
10. Psalm 119:29........................."the way of lying:"
11. Psalm 119:163........................"I hate and abhor lying:"
12. Psalm 120:2.."lying lips,"
13. Proverbs 6:17........ ...."a lying tongue,"
14. Proverbs 10:18............................"lying lips,"
15. Proverbs 12:19............................"lying tongue"
16. Proverbs 12:22............................"Lying lips are"
17. Proverbs 13:5............................"hateth lying:"
18. Proverbs 17:7........ ...."lying lips"
19. Proverbs 21:6........ ...."a lying tongue"
20. Proverbs 26:28........................"A lying tongue"
21. Isaiah 30:9............ ...."lying children,"
22. Isaiah 32:7.............. ...."lying words,"
23. Isaiah 59:13.......... ...."lying against the LORD,"
24. Jeremiah 7:4......................."Trust ye not in lying"
25. Jeremiah 7:8..............................."ye trust in lying"

26. Jeremiah 29:23.................."have spoken lying words"
27. Ezekiel 13:6..."lying divination,"
28. Ezekiel 13:7..."lying divination,"
29. Ezekiel 13:19..."by your lying"
30. Daniel 2:9........................"ye have prepared lying"
31. Hosea 4:2........................."By swearing, and lying,"
32. Jonah 2:8..........................."They that observe lying"
33. Ephesians 4:25..........................."putting away lying,"
34. 2 Thessalonians 2:9........"signs and lying wonders,"

Liar

1. Job 24:25..."make me a liar,"
2. Proverbs 17:4......................."and a liar giveth ear"
3. Proverbs 19:22..........................."better than a liar."
4. Proverbs 30:6..........................."thou be found a liar."
5. Jeremiah 15:18..........................."unto me as a liar,"
6. John 8:44.."for he is a liar,"
7. John 8:55..."I shall be a liar"
8. Romans 3:4..............................."every man a liar;"
9. 1 John 1:10..."make him a liar,"
10. 1 John 2:4..."is a liar,"
11. 1 John 2:22..."Who is a liar"
12. 1 John 4:20..."he is a liar:"
13. 1 John 5:10..........................."hath made him a liar;"

Liars

1. Deuteronomy 33:29...................."shall be found liars"
2. Psalm 116:11........................."All men are liars."
3. Isaiah 44:25..........................."the tokens of the liars,"
4. Jeremiah 50:36................."A sword is upon the liars;"
5. 1 Timothy 1:10..."for liars,"
6. Titus 1:12..................."Cretians are alway liars,"

7. Revelation 2:2......... ...."found them liars:"
8. Revelation 21:8......... ...."and all liars,"

Falsehood

1. 2 Samuel 18:13..................."have wrought falsehood"
2. Job 21:34.......... ...."there remaineth falsehood?"
3. Psalm 7:14.................."brought forth falsehood."
4. Psalm 119:118...... ...."their deceit is falsehood."
5. Psalm 144:8.................."right hand of falsehood."
6. Psalm 144:11...................."right hand of falsehood."
7. Isaiah 28:15..............................."and under falsehood"
8. Isaiah 57:4.......... ...."a seed of falsehood,"
9. Isaiah 59:13............. ...."words of falsehood."
10. Jeremiah 10:14............"molten image is falsehood,"
11. Jeremiah 13:25........ ...."trusted in falsehood."
12. Jeremiah 51:17............"molten image is falsehood,"
13. Hosea 7:1........................."for they commit falsehood;"
14. Micah 2:11.......... ...."in the spirit and falsehood"

False Witness

1. Exodus 20:16 ...."bear false witness"
2. Deuteronomy 5:20.........."false witness against thy"
3. Deuteronomy 19:16 ...."If a false witness rise up"
4. Deuteronomy 19:18...."witness be a false witness,"
5. Proverbs 6:19.................."false witness that speaketh"
6. Proverbs 12:17.................."but a false witness deceit."
7. Proverbs 14:5.................."false witness will utter lies."
8. Proverbs 19:5...... ...."false witness shall not be"
9. Proverbs 19:9...................."false witness shall not be"
10. Proverbs 21:28...... ...."false witness shall perish:"
11. Proverbs 25:18..... ...."false witness against his"
12. Matthew 15:19.............."false witness, blasphemies:"
13. Matthew 19:18........ ...."bear false witness,"

14. Matthew 26:59.............................."sought false witness"
15. Mark 10:19............................"Do not bear false witness,"
16. Mark 14:56...................."For many bare false witness"
17. Mark 14:57......... ...."and bare false witness"
18. Luke 18:20........................."Do not bear false witness,"
19. Romans 13:9.............................."bear false witness,"

False Lips
1.   Proverbs 17:4......................."giveth heed to false lips;"

False Tongue
1.   Psalm 120:3.."thou false tongue?"

NOTES

Notes

Notes